The Busy Mom's Guide:

HOW TO

SELL YOUR PASSION

*SEVEN PRINCIPLES TO SELL SEVEN FIGURES
FROM YOUR KITCHEN TABLE*

By

ELAINE TAN COMEAU

CEO & Founder of Easy Daysies®

Copyright © 2018 Elaine Tan Comeau

ISBN-13: 978-1-9804-9255-9

For information on special discounts for bulk purchases, please contact elaine@elaineskitchentable.com

For information on booking Elaine Tan Comeau as a speaker or author at your event, please contact elaine@elaineskitchentable.com

Front cover photo: Ron Comeau
Back cover photo: Ry Stars

With a Heart of Gratitude and Dedication

To God, in Whom I Can Do All Things (Phil. 4:13)

and

To Ron, the Man who makes my world spin,

To my Three Favorite Superheroes and my passion,
Abigail, Justin and Naomi,

and

To our Parents & Sisters who hold us up in every way,
Andrew & MaryAnn, Marcel & Muriel,
& Catherine, Michele, Niki, Rachele, and Ashlee

& to my Mompreneur Sisters, who know and live out the
certainty that we are stronger together

"Elaine came up with an idea at her kitchen table and she made a powerful impression on all five Dragons. She is one of those people who are born entrepreneurs. Elaine has a clear sense of how to move a product forward and where it could grow. Her passion is contagious, I mean, she's got me really interested in magnets! Elaine shares how passion can sell contagiously, in a simple and honest way."
- Jim Treliving, Owner and Chairman of Boston Pizza International, Founder of Treliving Management Services Ltd., Venture Capitalist, Television Personality and Investor on CBCs hit show Dragons' Den

"Elaine is a generous mother and a loving wife, and she brings the same warmth and personal attention to all her business relationships. There is no question that people want the product Elaine is selling. Her passion has led to countless sales, and she has the knowhow to show you how people will want to buy your product or services."
- Kevin O'Leary, Founder of O'Leary Ventures, Co-Founder and Chairman of O'Leary Funds, O'Leary Fine Wines, Investor, Best Selling Author, Financial Commentator, and TV Personality on ABC's popular entrepreneurial show Shark Tank

"Elaine clearly shares the simple yet brilliant ways that entrepreneurs can grow their sales exponentially. Such a great business resource and required reading for entrepreneurs (especially busy moms) at any level of business!"
- **Maria Locker, Founder & CEO, Mompreneur Showcase Group Inc.**

"I loved it and was super inspired. Elaine's advice is actionable and easy to track with her checklists and real life examples. Sell Your Passion will (re)ignite your passion for your business and put you back on course to greater success."
- **Wendy Armbruster, Founder & CEO, Snugabell**

CONTENTS

Get Bonus Materials for this book!

Follow this link and enter your email address for free future updates to this book and bonus materials for Sell Your Passion:

Go here:
www.ElainesKitchenTable.com/sellyourpassion

Get Free Audio Sessions for Entrepreneurial Success

At your own leisure, listen to secrets shared and interviews with successful individuals and experts who have done it, sold it, made it, marketed it, branded it, and now want to share it to help you and your business benefit, so that you can do the same!

Go here: www.ElainesKitchenTable.com

Introduction

Your business is merely a reflection of who you are - your thoughts, your heart, your mindset, your passion.

If we believe this, then business should be easy and selling should be even easier, right?

Nope.

Not at all.

However, I want you to know that selling <u>can</u> be easy. Selling can be effortless.

When what you do or have to offer encompasses all your passion, hopes, dreams, and intentions, it makes it so much easier to pull through every day, every failure, and every success.

Above all, what you have to offer becomes contagious.

Others will see your passion and, craving it for themselves, will want to share about it.

Often people have a great product or an incredible service to offer but they just cannot seem to sell it. Some people will say that they can't even give it away! Your situation may not be that dismal but you may just want to know how to sell a lot better than you are doing now. You will be happy to know that you picked up the right book. The principles I share have been tried and tested and will take you to levels of sales that will surprise you!

One of my mentors, Jim Treliving, once told me on my podcast *"Elaine's Kitchen Table...the Business of Real Life"** that "everyone is your mentor." Mentorship is the sharing of experience one offers after living through the peaks and valleys themselves. This is exactly what this book is for.

I strongly believe that we learn from each other no matter where each of us is in our own business journey. My hope is you will learn something from the principles of selling effortlessly as I share them within these pages, and from the lessons I have learned from my own mistakes and entrepreneurial journey. I am still learning something new every day.

I pray daily for my kids to have kind hearts and smart brains, and for them to wake up asking themselves two questions: One, what is something new I can learn today? And two, who can I help today?

I want to share my eureka moments with you in the hope that your own journey will be made easier.

Throughout this book I want you to take action.

---

*You can find my podcast at www.elaineskitchentable.com

You will not be a passive reader. In order to be different, you must think and behave differently.

If you want to be successful, it requires you to take action.

You are reading this book because you are a doer.

There is no trying. Just jump in and do it.

Here are the simple steps to get you in gear for the journey to success:

Step 1: Accountability

Right now, I would like you to think of someone you respect, someone who will always tell you the truth whether you want to hear it or not. Someone who will hold you accountable. I would like you to write their name here:

_____.

You need to call or text them right now and say: "[Name], I fully respect you and admire you. I am just starting to read a new book. It wants me to ask someone I respect and admire to hold me accountable to 'take action' in my business and life. I would be honored if you would be that person for me. There are only seven chapters in the book, so I would only check in with you seven times. Would this be okay with you? I would appreciate it so much!"

Step 2: Action

Each short chapter will share an empowerment quote and an action strategy. You will be held accountable for doing something to implement the strategy in your business since you are an action taker in your life and not a bystander.

A) Empowerment Quote – Every time you see an empowerment quote, I would like you to take a moment to write down what you are going to do about it. I want you to share the action that you are going to take with someone else. You can share it with your children, your spouse, your neighbor, your business partner, or a staff member. Why not motivate, challenge, or encourage someone else while you are at it? Lifting others up with you is a key principle I believe in and one you will see throughout this book.

B) Action Strategy to Sell – When you see an action strategy, get ready to roll up your sleeves. This is when you will think about your businesses and write down the following: 1. How you will apply this strategy to your business; 2. The goal you want to achieve with this strategy; and 3. A measurable result with a future date of accomplishment. Then you will share this action strategy and all three corresponding points with the person you chose in Step 1.

Step 3: Achieve and Amaze

What is the point of accomplishing a task, reaching a goal, discovering an incredible solution or answer to a problem, if you cannot share it to make a positive difference in someone else's life? Is helping improve the life of another not the reason for all that we do? Then you need to share it, and share it boldly. It is your duty to amaze, help, rescue, and liberate others with the solution(s) you have discovered!

When we think of our product or service, we must think of its purpose, its message, and how it is able to help our customer or client. What are the benefits that we are offering that others need to know about? What is this incredible gift it offers that nothing or no-one else does or can do? This is what you are "selling." When you believe in it and can genuinely prove it works, then do not be shy or selfish about it—share it passionately! This book is meant to be your kick in the butt to take action on what you have achieved and get you to boldly amaze the world!

You have got this!

If you are reading this book, you definitely have a lot of one of my favorite words: gumption. Gumption is the ability to do something with determination, resourcefulness, spunk, and energy, to just keep going, picking yourself up each time you fall, moving forward until your goal is achieved.

Quick story: I originally wanted to call this book #GotGumption but it did not win the vote. So please do put that hashtag in your heart and tattoo it on your mind, and remember you have got gumption. You will amaze the world, starting with yourself!

CEO after CEO will share that successful people do something they are passionate about, something they love.

Success is doing what you love and being able to effectively communicate it and share it with others. This book will share seven principles to achieve exactly that. You do not need to apply all seven, but you will find at least one principle that will be your eureka moment.

I cannot wait for that to happen for you! Go ahead and start your adventure. (I am holding the door open for you.)

Chapter One:
Principle #1 – Be on Purpose

Empowerment Quote:

The purpose of life is not to be happy but to matter, to be useful, and to have in some way made a difference that you lived at all.
— Ralph Waldo Emerson

What does this mean to you and what are you going to do about it?

Mark Twain so eloquently stated that, "The two most important days in your life are the day you are born and the day you find out why." Perhaps, we have been asking children to focus on the wrong concept when growing up, which can make us stuck as adults. We often hear people ask children, "What do you want to be when you grow up?" We are asking them the wrong question. This question sets them up to focus on the wrong goal in life. Instead, we should be asking children, "What kind of impact or footprint do you want to leave on our planet?" Or if they are too young for that question, "How do you want to help people when you grow up?" You see, the first question focuses on *a job*. The second focuses on *a purpose*.

The first question makes children focus on the end result, on the superficial—the corner office, the shiny red fire truck, the title of doctor, lawyer, teacher, dentist, baker, banker, pilot, and so on. There is absolutely nothing wrong with titles or corner offices, but what is most important is the meaning behind *why* we do *what* we do. If there is no meaning, we move on from job to job. And perhaps this is why studies show that a person will change jobs an average of seven times in their lifetime. I have seen teachers who teach but do not like teaching, or even children for that matter. I have seen lawyers dislike law and become teachers. I have seen accountants become chefs. I have seen chefs become truck and bus drivers. You will know you are doing the right job when you simply love doing what you do.

The second question, "What kind of impact or footprint do you want to leave on our planet?" demands something deeper, for that true purpose belonging uniquely to each one of us. When you know what your purpose is, it is a wonderful thing to make it evident in all you do. When you know your purpose, you cannot help but make everything you do *be on purpose*, to make some difference that you existed at all.

Be on purpose.

What problem does your product or service solve? What solution do you provide to an existing problem? For me it was that when I was a school teacher, so many parents asked me to help their children be better listeners, to help their children become more independent and cooperative in their day. Year after year, parents would ask me to make a visual schedule for their kids at home, similar to the one I had made for the front of my classroom, to help their child get out the door faster in the morning. So, I did. I drew these schedules simple enough for non-readers to feel confident with their day, whether they were two or twelve years old. For me, my purpose began with my heart's desire to help children have easier days.

I had the honor of beginning my teaching career in inner-city schools. My very first class was a grade two class where almost all of my seven-year-olds were latch-key kids. I did not have one married family in my class, and several of the moms were prostitutes. Sometimes parents would show up drunk to pick up their children. Often, my students walked home on their own, trying to steer clear of the gang outside that was recruiting the grade five and six students. I would see these seven-year-olds go get their younger brother or sister from kindergarten and then go home. They would have burn marks on their forearms from making dinner for themselves over the stove. My heart broke for these kids.

As often as I could, I would make sure to pack extra food, granola bars, and extra socks and mittens, especially during the cold winters in Toronto, to pass on to some of them. Some of these kids would bring Diet Coke and Doritos for lunch because that was what mom had at home.

The children in my class each year had so much working against them. Studies show that one in four school age children comes to school with anxiety issues, one in five with learning disabilities (according to The National Institute of Health), one in two from broken families, one in forty-eight is on the Autism spectrum, one in five has mental health issues, and it goes on and on. When statistics show that children have so much working against them, I knew that I had a tool to help children achieve confidence and busy families to de-stress. I made my visual schedules by parent demand for years and years—and for free. I loved my students and their families. I fell in love with my class every year. My grade two class even sang at our wedding.

You see, it begins with my first principle: **Be on Purpose.**

Ralph Waldo Emerson, in the 1800s, wrote that, "The purpose of life is not to be happy but to matter, to be productive, to be useful, to have it make some difference that you have lived at all." So, ask yourself, what is your purpose? What is the difference you want to make in the world? What is the footprint you want to leave behind?

If you are a realtor, your purpose is not to sell real estate, but it may be that you truly and strongly believe that every person has the right to find and own a beautiful and comfortable home that they love and feel safe in.

If you sell makeup, your purpose is not to sell lipstick, but it may be that you passionately believe that every woman needs to know how beautiful she is and confidently shine in her own special way. You are going to help them find that sparkle.

Are you ready to hear the golden nugget, the secret behind the principle of "Be on purpose" that will make the most impactful change in not only the way you sell, think, and behave, but also in your sales results? Here it is:

First, ask yourself what your purpose is, and once you know what it is, and you understand that is *why* you do what you do, then you can answer the next and most important question.

Your ability to answer this next question will change all that you do from now on in your business. If you can answer this question, you will be successful and you will sell effortlessly and contagiously.

Here is the question of all questions: How is what you offer (your product or service) an extension of that purpose?

If you can answer this question, you will be able to sell successfully, effortlessly and contagiously.

I am not asking about the purpose of your product or service, but rather of your existence. In this book, you are not a passive reader but an active contributor to your own learning, and I would like you to actually write down your answers and be held accountable for them. Studies show that goals are 80% more likely to happen when you write them down. Do it.

What is your purpose and how is what you do or offer an extension of that purpose?

If you do not know how to answer this question then you are most likely having trouble selling your product or service. Do not despair. You just need to ask yourself why your service or product is an extension of what your core values and beliefs are. Write them down. You'll have your eureka moment when you do.

Action Strategy #1: Be On Purpose

Think about your business and write down:

1. How will you apply this principle to your business?
2. What is the promise you want to achieve with this strategy?
3. What is the measurable result you want, with a date of accomplishment?
4. Share this action strategy and all three parts above with the person you chose to hold you accountable in the introduction of this book.

Chapter Two: Principle #2 – Be a "Triple Threat"

Empowerment Quote:

Success is liking who you are, liking what you do, and liking how you do it.

—Maya Angelou

What does this mean to you and what are you going to do about it?

My husband often says, "Life is like sports." This is the moment where I will let him say, *I told you so.* Or even better, I think he would appreciate it more if I said, "Honey, you are right." I did marry the smartest and kindest man I know.

Early on in my teaching career, I had the privilege of being the grade 7 boys' basketball coach. Yes, little, brand new, twenty-four-year-old me. I was just assigned my first ever kindergarten class of 22 four and five-year-olds, and also, that same September, I was told that I *had* to coach the grade seven boys' basketball team, a group of 22 twelve-year-old boys. I was terrified. I did not know which to be more afraid of!

Both opportunities yanked me right out of my comfort zone, both taught me survival skills, and both introduced me to my love of coffee (and Tylenol, but not at the same time). Both inspired me to research and develop new-found skill sets, and both imparted on me incredible lessons I now implement in life, in business, and in sales.

I quickly learned that each group spoke a "different language." I had to shift gears throughout the day when I saw each group, and also use different tones of voice (high pitched bubbly to the kindergarteners, and happy firm tone to the basketball team). To be successful with both groups, I had to have a confident, caring persona, one that would let them know I was in charge and in control, even though sometimes I had no idea what I was doing. This was the best training for *ingenuity.* This was preparing me for the many hats I would wear as an entrepreneur and lay the foundation for some serious sales mastery.

I coached grade 7 boys basketball for five years. I did not know how to play basketball. My principal told me that since I was the new teacher I had to coach the grade 7 boys' basketball team or else there would not be a team at all. So, of course I said yes!

When the boys kept asking me what position they would be playing and what plays we would be doing, I quickly learned all I could about basketball from borrowing videos from the local library. I still did not know how to play basketball or perform a lay-up for the life of me, but I could speak the language and could plan strategic plays that would cause my team to win game after game. I quickly discovered that the point guard would pick and roll and drive the ball up the post and alley-oop.

I implemented what I learned, created three power plays, and my team of 22 boys won the district finals that first year! May I add that I was the only *female* boys' basketball coach in the district finals that year?

I learned that I had to *sell* my genuine passion for wanting the boys to do well, and that I was in it with all my heart. Kids are amazingly intuitive; if they know you don't want to be there, they don't want to be there either. My team knew I wanted to be there for each and every practice and for each and every game. They knew I was proud of them and that I just wanted them to try their best and have fun. They knew I also wanted our team to win.

My passion translated into the boys wanting to do their best and sell their skills to any team we played. That is contagious passion. I will touch more on selling contagiously in Chapter Seven. Our customers and clients are the same. They are very intuitive. They know if you are fully in, *they know if you believe in what you are offering,* and if they sense that you aren't or don't, they will leave you.

It is true that everything you need to know in life you learned in kindergarten: how to share, how to take turns, to wash your hands (often), to flush, to ask before taking something, to put things back where you got them, and so on. All necessary survival skills for the social world we live in.

Basketball teaches team work, how to work on and build on personal and group strengths and weaknesses, how to pick yourself up and keep moving forward even when the odds are against you, how to win with grace and humility, and how to show sportsmanship honorably when the win does not happen. The skills of training and sportsmanship transfer to the professional and business worlds too.

The basketball skill that best describes the character and charm of an incredibly successful business owner and entrepreneur is the "triple threat." Triple threat means that you are in a comfortable stance where you get a moment to think about what you are going to do and you have three options: to shoot, to pass, or to drive it forward.

Let's break it down and compare how each of these moves makes you ready to sell at your best. At one point, you will find that you have a choice to make: to go for the close and sell it, to pass the opportunity to someone else for now, or to drive it forward to do your best no matter the outcome.

The Triple Threat Position

This triple threat position is not a passive stance. This is when you are in a position to make a potential sale, where you are actively thinking, researching comparing, and forecasting. This is when you are about to make a very impactful decision that will decide how a possible successful sale will close, and when.

Basketball is a fast-moving game, and it is powerful to see how fast the pro NBA players handle their triple threat positions. They make quick decisions because they already know and can predict their teammates' moves, and if they are really good, they can predict their opponents' moves too. In the minor leagues and in grade 7 basketball, the triple threat stance is more deliberate, evident, and methodical. You can see the thinking happening and eyes darting as the player searches for someone to pass to, a clear path to drive forward, or an opening to make a clear shot.

In business, we start off like the grade 7 player, and as we get more and more experience, we begin to have faster reaction time during our triple threat stances and make quicker and smarter decisions.

Being in a triple threat position is the moment you take the sales conversation and decide whether you are going to go for the close and "shoot," or you realize that this client does not have the same core values and you would not be the right fit so you "pass" on the deal, or you discover that there is great potential with this possible client and you are going to do your best to develop a relationship and "drive it forward" because you can see it resulting in a sale.

When you study the posture of a professional in the triple threat stance, this is what you want to mirror: He leans in, with his strongest foot forward, ready to move quickly and confidently. Just as in business, we can ruin a good opportunity if we start off with a weak idea or bad product, or start too soon.

I was once too eager to get my products into a large national retailer. I was not ready; my manufacturing was not secure and the product was an imperfect first run with a new manufacturer. The product did well and became a best seller instantly, but I could not properly fulfill a re-order and then lost the shelf space for that account. That was a weak foot I leapt off of, and I ended up falling. I learned very quickly that the only thing better than an order is a re-order.

The professional has his knees bent, back straight, head up, eyes looking at where he is going next. Likewise in business, we need to have our head up, seeing what competitors are up to, what the trends are, what is coming up against us, and who is around that we can possibly work with, collaborate with, or sell to.

The major benefit of the triple threat is to protect the ball, and review the options available. In business, it forces you to stop and think, to look for opportunities, to calm yourself, and to find the target. It is a chance to think about your next move, to exhibit patience. You want to be comfortable so that you can move in any position. Now let's talk about sales specifically.

Drive It Forward

Because you were in a triple threat position, you were able to spot a possible new prospect. We know that all good business begins with establishing a relationship. Like in dating, we have to get to know each other. On the one hand, your potential client or customer wants to know your story, your core values, and why you do what you do. They want to know about the product or service you have to offer them.

On the other (more important) hand, the potential customer wants to know what is in it for them. *They want to know what problem you are going to solve in their lives.* How are you going to make their lives better or easier, save them money, or make them money?

When you take time to build a rapport with your customers or potential customer, you can truly help them. This is where your passion will shine through your service, through your product, and through the solution you are going to provide for them because you truly heard their need.

Effectively listening to your potential client may even require you to show them what their real problem is, and hopefully it is one that you can solve.

What I mean here is that I listen to people share about things going on in their lives, how exhausted they are in the mornings, exasperated with yelling at their kids, frustrated with being tuned out, drained from meltdowns and tantrums, and tired of nagging. They think that the problem is that their kids won't listen. Indeed, the number one question parents ask me is, "How do I get my kids to listen?"

Being ready, in my triple treat position, I am on my strong foot ready to push off and help them. Being ready means I have already done the research and know the solution, the rebuttals, and the possible alternatives and competitors. I hear what they say is their problem and I hear the solutions they have tried in vain.

Then I share back what I have heard so that they know they have been listened to and are understood. I continue by sharing that the solutions they have been trying do not work because they are not dealing with the true problem.

The true problem is not that their kids will not listen to them. Rather, we want to solve the problem of how to get kids to do what they are supposed to do. I share with them that studies show that over 80% of a child's learning is visual. The reality is that a very low percentage of children learn from just auditory learning alone. Now we can begin to understand why talking ourselves blue in the face does not make things better, and move on to a more effective solution.

Bottom line, your potential buyer/client/investor, wants to know how this relationship with you is going to benefit them.

When you have established the following check list, you can move forward and build a healthy relationship with this person, group, or company, knowing that it will result in the close of a sale, and most likely a referral to another one.

Drive It Forward	Check
They have a problem that you can solve with your service(s) or product(s)	Yes
They fit your customer avatar / profile	Yes
You want to work with them	Yes

In Kevin O'Leary's book *Cold Hard Truth on Family, Kids, & Money* I shared how important people's relationships are. I shared that I would always bake cookies to bring with orders that I delivered. For me, *driving it forward* is about building relationships and not just closing the deal. Some of my first retailers still talk about how I am the only vendor they have ever met that brings them homemade cookies and they will always remember that. Kevin jokes that although this works for me, you will never see him bring freshly baked cookies to a business meeting. I do that because it is who I am.

Driving it forward is about being confident enough to pursue the sale with poise and grace.

Confidence is the ability to move forward with certainty, not in the pending outcome or the present circumstance, but certainty in yourself, in your product or service, and in your passions and beliefs. I knew that I had a proven product with Easy Daysies and I was still surprised when several retailers told me that I should take Easy Daysies on the investor television show called *Dragons' Den*. It was after a toy trade show where one retailer asked me if I could sell her 8000 units. I knew that it took me a year to make around 2000 units off my kitchen table, but I did not want to say no. She took me by the hand and said that I needed to get off my kitchen table and go on a show like *Dragons' Den*.

After we flew home from the trade show, my husband was on the computer and he turned to me and said, "Elaine, *Dragons' Den* auditions are here in town on Saturday!" It was Thursday. I knew it was a now or never moment. I only told my in-laws and my parents that I was going to pitch on the *Den*. Even though I had just spent four days pitching my product to retailers, I knew this pitch would have to be different.

I knew that I had to nail it in the first 60 seconds and that those first 60 seconds would have to captivate the investors and tell them how it could make them money. I had to *sell* Easy Daysies like I had never sold Easy Daysies before. For the next 48 hours I practiced and fine-tuned over and over what I would say. I also had to know my numbers—my projections for the next year, three years, and five years. I knew I had to be able to answer any question thrown at me.

I also knew the importance of the story behind Easy Daysies. I often share when I am on stage talking about marketing and selling that the most important differentiator about your company, your product, or your service is the story behind it. You are the only one with that story. There may be many kinds of tires, shoes, baby diapers, or pasta sauce, but what separates you from the rest is your story of how and why you sell what you sell.

I was nervous, as a startup business, but I knew that this was my opportunity to *drive it forward*.

If you would like to know more about how my little family and I auditioned, got a call back to fly out to Toronto to film our pitch in front of the five Dragons, how we incited a bidding war between all five investors, and how we secured both Kevin O'Leary and Jim Treliving as our partners, please do check out my podcast at http://www.elaineskitchentable.com (episodes 11, 12 and 13).

Driving it forward means going for it, knowing confidently who you want to sell to and going boldly for the close, with gumption.

Realize that it is okay to stumble along the way, or to encounter road blocks. All this means is that you get to stop and get into triple threat position again. It's all good. And just like in sports, you will not get better if you just sit on the sidelines and don't practice.

Being unable to check all three points on the Drive It Forward Chart takes us to our next triple threat action.

Pass It

A simple and often forgotten Sales 101 lesson is that not everyone is our customer. As fabulous as we think our product is, it should not be for everyone, or it won't really help anyone. And although we may believe we have a service useful to every living person, that is simply not the case.

Not every opportunity is a good opportunity, either.

We must ask ourselves, is this someone we want our company to be associated with? Can our product or service actually solve an existing problem they have? Be proud of what you have to offer; it is special, and that means that it is not supposed to be for everyone.

To sum it up quickly, the same chart we just used can be used here to make the point of why you need to move on and pass on this sale.

Pass It	Check
They have a problem that you can solve with your service(s) or product(s)	No
They fit your customer avatar / profile	No
You want to work with them	No

No matter what you have to offer, if it cannot help that person or company, you cannot sell to them. But what makes you memorable is if you can pass them on to someone you trust and know who *can* help them. When you do this, even though you did not get a sale, they will most likely refer you to someone else who *does* need your product or service. This is the best *pass*, one that results in the guaranteed referral based on your character. This *pass* also demonstrates the same passion you would have demonstrated through providing your product or service.

We have all played with the simple wooden puzzles where we slide the shapes into the corresponding shape slot. A square piece cannot fit in a triangle slot. Similarly, we cannot sell to someone who clearly does not fit the shape of our customer avatar. Your avatar is a character equivalent of your ideal customer, your specific target market client. You will know when someone is not your avatar when you have to work super hard to explain why they need your product or service. The right customer does not need to be convinced.

Sometimes you will have a client who has the money to buy from you, but they might not even need your product or know what it is, or they may be very critical and misunderstand it. This is a customer who may take up a lot of your time to convince that they need your product. You have options here: to pass them to one of your team members, or to pass on them completely.

Take the Shot

This action is when you go with your gut. You know that you can close the deal. Everything feels right. There is no uneasy feeling. Everything is lined up perfectly for you to take the shot. As Wayne Gretzky says, "You miss 100% of the shots you don't take."

Going for a confident close is very similar to the "Drive it Forward" chart, with one key difference: Rather than you wanting to work with them, it is clear that *they want to work with you.*

Here is the chart for those who are visual learners like me:

Take the Shot and Close the Sale	Check
They have the problem that you can certainly solve with your service(s) or product(s)	Yes
They do fit your exact customer avatar or profile	Yes
They want to work with you	Yes

This can be one of those wonderful moments where the customer cold-calls you! The customer comes to you and tells you they need and want your product and then pay you for it. You still need to make sure that you are in triple threat position so that you can see it coming and not miss the opportunity. Being in triple threat means being ready to serve, to fulfill the order, to make that meeting happen, to follow up and follow through. The worst feeling is to lose a sale because you did not follow through and the customer says, "You never got back to me so I went somewhere else."

We have to cherish these customers, the ones who come to you, the ones who desired your service or product first without you even pitching to them. These are the customers who can and will be wonderful word-of-mouth envoys, ambassadors, and raging fans. Treat them well, show them gratitude, and ask for their testimonials.

I am always so honored and grateful when I receive an order for Easy Daysies. It is humbling and thrilling to walk into a store like Staples and see my products in their PDQ year after year. I have the same thrill and exhilaration when I walk into a wonderful independent education, book, or toy store, like Education Station or Odin Books, and see Easy Daysies on their shelves. It is truly such an honor.

I sought out my first retailers myself because obviously nobody had heard of my new product. After establishing a reputation, retailers would approach my booth at a trade show and say, "OK, my friend from XYZ store sent me here and said I have to check out your product." These were pre-qualified leads coming straight to me and asking for me to take my shot! By our fourth year, Easy Daysies was available in about 1500 stores across North America.

When you live out your passion, all sorts of people are

drawn to you. Sometimes the right type of customer is attracted to you, and sometimes not.

You do not need to sell to everyone who wants buy from you. You can say no.

I have learned to say no to some large and small partnerships because I did not see my products as a fit for a certain store, or I knew it would not sell well there.

I recall one of the first stores to ever order Easy Daysies. I was very excited! It was local so I went to visit the store to personally deliver the order and upon seeing the store I knew that my product would not be a good fit. I want the store to be successful in selling my products and not have a hard time with my product taking up their precious shelf space. So, I reduced the size of their order to make sure that they would sell through. I told the owner that she could place a re-order when she sold through. The store owner was very grateful for my suggestion.

I have said no to a partnership with a very large dollar store chain because I did not see my product as a dollar store item. It would have been a good sized order, but that was not in alignment with my brand.

It is important to go with your gut and not your heart in matters of business transactions. To quote one of my mentors and *Dragons' Den* partners, Jim Treliving: "I make decisions about work with my heart, about money with my head, and about people with my gut. ... I like to listen to my gut when it comes to hiring and partnering."

This is worth repeating in a chart:

Area of Business:	Make Decisions With:
Money	Head
Work	Heart
People	Gut

I learned this lesson the hard way. I believe that I work smart and cautiously when it comes to moving forward with new partnerships, yet I still made a very costly mistake, one that I will share here so that you can learn from the example.

There was a distributor from France who wrote to me sharing his interest in partnering with Easy Daysies. At first I did not reply to his e-mails, thinking they may be spam. He persisted with his e-mails. I finally replied thanking him for his interest and shared that I was focusing on distribution in North America at that time and would get back to him when I was ready. He continued to email me for a year and a half. He would share photos of his four-year-old son with me and try to connect with me on a personal level. I fell for it—he was pulling on my heart strings. I sent his son chocolates from Canada and he kept sending me occasional photos.

He shared that since we had been corresponding for about a year and a half that I should be able to trust him, and so I agreed. He placed a large enough order with me to justify my hiring a company to translate my product into international French.

Just when the order was manufactured and ready to ship from China, he told me he had to cancel the order. This was shocking to me. To make a long story much shorter, he made me believe that it would help him if he could receive my products and pay on net terms because his business and family were having unforeseen financial problems. He said that having my products to sell would help their cash flow and get them back on their feet.

My gut told me not to do it. But my heart unfortunately made the decision to not cancel and let the order ship. The net term date came and went, with no payment. Over the following months there were a few calls and many excuses, but no money. For two years I would try to get my payment even though the French distributor had long since stopped replying to me. I lost sleep over this for almost that entire time. What bothered me the most was that his company's website and social media continued to use photos of my children to sell my product that he never paid for.

This very costly example taught me two vital business sales lessons: 1. Do not ever make decisions about people in business with my heart but rather to trust my gut; and 2. Get paid 100% up-front on first time orders. I may have saved a lot of money since that incident by implementing these policies.

So remember, just because someone wants to buy your product or service or wants to work with you, it does not mean that you have to.

Action Strategy #2: Be a Triple Threat

Think about your businesses and write down:

1. How will you apply this principle to your business?

2. What is the promise you want to achieve with this strategy?

3. What is the measurable result you want, with a date of accomplishment?

4. Share this action strategy and all three parts above with the person you chose to hold you accountable in the introduction of this book.

SELL YOUR PASSION

Chapter Three:
Principle #3 – Be a Doer

Empowerment Quote:

You must do the things you think you cannot. — Eleanor Roosevelt

What does this mean to you and what are you going to do about it?

There is a great saying that goes like this: *"At first they will ask you why you are doing it—then they will ask you how you did it." (Author Unknown)*

When you first started out doing what you do or selling what you sell, you probably had doubters commenting on your misjudgment of giving up a secure job to do what you are doing now (or, if you are reading this in anticipation of starting something new, you may be the one asking yourself those questions).

Perhaps they gave you advice to stop now and that it is not too late to get your real job back. Or maybe they questioned how you will survive doing what you do, or doubted anyone would even need what you offer. You see, it is true that *those who are crazy enough to think they can change the world usually do*. I believe someone from Apple named Steve Jobs shared that brilliant comment.

When I was a school teacher, I would start the school year by telling my students to always reach for the stars, because even if you fall, you will still land higher than where you started. Reach for the stars and let your passion—your *why*—be your fuel!

The paramount principle we need to understand and incorporate before we can be a *doer* is the following: When you make it known that the service or product you are offering is simply *an extension* of your passion, your prospective client or customer will *know* your why. This is the principle we need to understand and translate into how we sell. Your passion *is* your *why*.

We need to understand how what we offer is part of our passion—our *why*. Then, we need to successfully convey that message to the rest of the world.

Science shows that when you write goals and thoughts down, you have a more complete understanding, that your whole body will actually physiologically help make it happen rather than it being lost in your subconscious. Jot down here how you believe that *your* service or product is an extension of your passion, your purpose, your *why*:

Once we know and believe in our passion and purpose, we are ready to go out and *do*. Having passion is not just the spark required to want to do something great and wonderful, but rather it is the fuel that keeps us going, especially when we feel like we are running on empty. Your passion—your *why*—is vital to the health and longevity of your sales and business lifespan.

Why Do We Not Do

Walt Disney says: *"The way to get started is to quit talking and begin doing."* However, why is it that some of us don't just run out there and share our passion?

1. *We Don't Love It, So Choose What You Love*

First of all, I am going to replace the word "sell" with the word "offer." Loving and believing in what you offer makes it so much easier to sell to others. So, if you do not have that going for you right now, please do yourself a favour and stop selling it. This book is about selling your passion, not someone else's.

I am often in awe of the wisdom I get from chatting with my Uber drivers on the way to meetings in different cities. As I headed to a big meeting in Boca Raton, Florida, for which I had just flown twelve hours across the country from another country, feeling butterflies in my core from nervousness, my wise Haitian driver, Frecin, said, "You have to love what you do. When you have passion for what you do, it just shines right through you." Exactly.

Your passion becomes your *why*. I love what I do. My passion is two-fold when it comes to my work. I have a passion to help children, busy families, and adults (with early memory loss) have easier and better quality days through my product line called Easy Daysies®. I also have a passion to come alongside other women entrepreneurs as I strongly believe and hold true to the motto of *"We are stronger together."*

I love to learn and I love to share the lessons I have learned in my journey in the hope that it will make the journey for others easier and faster. On any given week, especially when it was near audition time for the TV shows *Dragons' Den* and *Shark Tank*, I would receive e-mails and phone calls from women who asked if they could take me out for coffee to "pick my brain."

As much as I love coffee and helping other women, it was a challenge to keep meeting complete strangers for three hours in my day when I have three kids and a business to run. This led to the creation of my podcast for women entrepreneurs called *Elaine's Kitchen Table... the Business of Real Life*, and it also led to me owning and running the Mompreneurs Canada chapter for Vancouver & Greater Vancouver, British Columbia. I had the honor of winning the 2014 Canadian Mompreneur of the Year, and then became their first ambassador before I took on the chapter two years later.

The podcast got its name from the fact that I started my business off my kitchen table and still proudly choose to work from there as it is the closest place to my family. You can check it out here: http://www.elaineskitchentable.com/iTunes

2. We Lack Confidence, Not Ability

Studies show that two out of the next three small businesses in North America will be started by women and that, of that group, two thirds will be moms.

Women, did you know that you are a natural selling expert? It is largely because you are also a natural buying expert. About 80-85% of household purchasing decisions are made by women. In fact, women control about 12 trillion of the 18.4 trillion dollars of global consumer spending, according to many studies including the *Boston Consulting Group* and *The Singapore Business Times.*

We are a growing force to be taken seriously, but it begins by taking ourselves seriously. We all have that voice telling us we cannot do it, we are not good enough, we are not smart enough. But you know what? You are the expert!

I have interviewed a lot of amazing people on my podcast. Several successful business women have shared this same valuable example. When shown a list of criteria for a job, a woman will take a look at it, see the one thing she *cannot* do and then say that she is not qualified for the job. A man, on the other hand, will look at the same list, see the one thing he *can* do and then say that he is qualified for the job. Women, we have no reason not to have the same assertiveness and be confident in our incredible abilities rather than in our possible inabilities.

We would get things done so much faster if we put our energy into DOING rather than spending time focusing on what we think we cannot do. Some of my brilliant mentors—Jim, Kevin, Alex, Brad, Jason, Nancy and Ron (yes, almost all men)—have taught me that you need to recognize what your strengths are and what your weaknesses are. Then, hire or partner with someone else who has those strengths so you can focus on what you are best at for your business.

That is what we are going to do. We are going to hold each other accountable for DOING and SUCCEEDING—that is why I created this book! If you want something, talk about it, write it down, and keep talking about it while you take action steps toward it.

How Do We Do It

1. *Talk About It and Write About It*

A wise and generous mentor, Jason, once told me that if you want to do something, talk about it. Someone who is listening may be able to help you or knows someone who can help you. Studies show that people who write their goals down are 80% more likely to accomplish them, and yet only about 3% of us in North America do that. Wow, what an easy opportunity to become one of the 3% who is most likely to succeed!

Writing your sales goals down with timelines keeps you accountable to achieve them. If you cannot measure it, it does not exist! You have got this. You can make money doing what you love doing.

I want you to hold yourself accountable for your own success. The key step to achieving that success is to *be a doer*. You need to show up daily for yourself by *doing*. Schedule it in your daily calendar that you will work *on* your business, not *in* your business, each morning for two hours. Read, study, and learn how to improve the way you do business, how you sell, how you have systemized your sales calls, and follow up. Also, schedule two hours where you work solely on income generating tasks (sales!), because being busy in work does not mean you are making money.

You make money by selling your offerings; that is, your products and/or services.

More and more women are becoming leaders. I think what sets us apart as mom-entrepreneurs is that we do not only see ourselves as business leaders but as role models to our children.

On my podcast in the summer of 2015, I had the pleasure of interviewing Kevin O'Leary. He stated that of the 27 private companies he was investing in (Easy Daysies Ltd. included), the only ones returning a profit were those run by women. He finished by saying, *"If you want something done, give it to a busy mom."*

According to Industry Canada, 47% of small to mid-sized businesses are entirely or partly owned by women. These businesses represent over $117 *billion* in economic activity in Canada.

According to the National Association of Women Business Owners, more that 9.1 million firms in the USA are women-owned and generate more than 1.5 trillion dollars in sales. Women-owned business in the USA account for 31% of all privately owned businesses. Women-owned businesses make up one in five firms with a revenue of $1 million or more.

Why is this female shift in business happening? I believe there are two main reasons:

A) North American families generally need two incomes to survive. Mothers are choosing to be their own boss so they can spend time with their children while making money on their own terms.

B) Who knows better what a woman wants (remember, women are deciding how to spend $4 out of every $5 in the consumer economy) than a woman?

2. *Do Give Gratitude*

Begin by giving daily gratitude. We have nothing if we do not have gratitude. Make it a priority to show gratitude to your clients and partners. What or who are you grateful for right now and why? Write it down.

Make a point to set aside time to thank *three people daily* through e-mails, e-cards, or mailed cards. These people could be your future clients, staff, or other professional colleagues.

There is nothing too small to be grateful for. What is amazing is that when we show gratitude, even for the smallest things, the results are hugely impactful. Sending a thank you card or taking the time to write an e-mail to thank someone touches them personally. Your kind effort of appreciation will go a long way.

I have had many experiences where opportunities present themselves based on someone to whom I showed gratitude many months and even years prior—all because the person was impacted by the gratitude I showed.

Remember, people do not remember what you say or what you do, but they will always remember how you made them feel.

It is also good to give gratitude to those who give you negative feedback on your offerings. Thank them for sharing and let them know you always appreciate any feedback as product quality and customer satisfaction are of utmost importance to you and your company. Plus, you can put their feedback into consideration for improvement where needed. When your customer feels heard, you have given them a good feeling of being valued. They will remember that feeling perhaps more than what they did not like about your product or service.

1. *Start with a Simple Tool for Sales Success*

On the next page you will find a sales tracking guide for you to copy and use. Write down your sales challenge for the week. For example, I may write down: "Get Easy Daysies into a new mass retailer" or "Book two speaking events for July" (remember, you must be ready to fulfill your sales goals, so your goals must be accomplishable).

Then write out two goals that you will accomplish this week that will take you toward achieving your sales challenge. For example, my first goal may be to get my products into Staples Canada. I would write "Staples" in my Goal #1 box as my first goal, and another mass retailer in my Goal #2 box. Then as my Action Step I would write: "Research and contact buyers with the press release telling of Easy Daysies being named Top Ten Most Innovative Small Businesses in 2018 in British Columbia." A great result to fill in would be "Received e-mail reply and have meeting set for month, day, year, time." Write it down, get it done, make money.

From Sales Challenge to Sales Growth

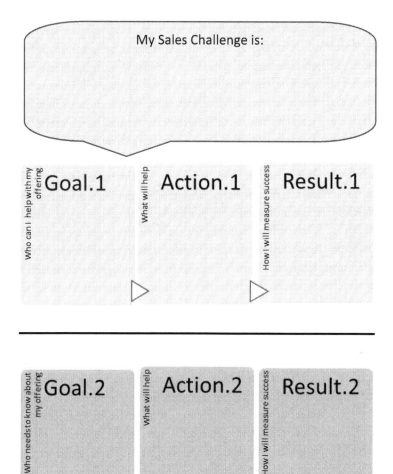

Elaine Tan Comeau Copyright 2018

Action Strategy #3: Be a Doer.

Think about your businesses and write down:

1. How will you apply this principle to your business?

2. What is the promise you want to achieve with this strategy?

3. What is the measurable result you want, with a date of accomplishment?

4. Share this action strategy and all three parts above with your accountability partner you chose in the introduction of this book.

In my garage with a shipment of Easy Daysies – low overheads help!

Spotting Easy Daysies at Staples Canada.

Always a thrill to see Easy Daysies in the media!
(photo courtesy Breakfast Television)

Top: Our daughter handing Easy Daysies to Arlene Dickinson and Kevin O'Leary on the CBC hit show Dragons' Den (photo courtesy CBC Dragons' Den). Other photos – a collage of time with the CBC Dragons and producers.

Podcasting in our home office. www.elaineskitchentable.com

Spotting Easy Daysies at Walmart but it was sold out!
And once again a year later at Walmart!

After a mentor-meeting with the wonderful Jim Treliving. Holding our new
My Day for adults with early memory loss issues.

My first Achieve & Lead Women's Conference that I hosted in 2016.
It was the biggest event I planned since my wedding!

I love speaking to teachers at Professional Development Days! Teachers are
so very special to me. They have such an important and impactful job. And
teachers are always selling their passion in their classroom.

An example of three beautiful friends in my life who dropped what they were doing to help me at a time of need across the country!

With some of the great minds (Kevin O'Leary and his right-hand man Alex) at their offices. That's me sitting at Kevin's desk!

A family that works together... my oldest helping her mama.

Our parents hold us together and made us who we are, they are who I aspire to be like. Ron and I were blessed to have them here as Easy Daysies Ltd. was awarded the Chamber of Commerce Business Excellence Award.

It takes a village of amazing friends and family that surprise you at your door to help you get ready to assemble hundreds of goodies for the 39th Annual Emmy Awards Swag Bag and then they stick around to see what else they can help you with and assemble all sorts of products and displayers for you without you even asking! (Because they know I don't like to ask for help). Can you spot the famous Kitchen Table where it all began?

Our little family on Dragons Den, Season 6! We just pitched! Can you tell by our smiles that we got a deal? We then became known as one of the Top Five Most Heartwarming Pitches on the Den and were invited to tape three more updates! Maybe there will be a fourth – stay tuned!

We love spotting Easy Daysies in stores! - Chapters Indigo

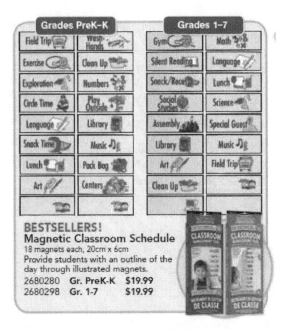

A dream come true! As a child and as a school teacher, I loved Scholastic Books! It was a dream for me to one day have a product in Scholastic, but being a Best Seller is beyond my dream come true!

Our little family just after the first Easy Daysies product was launched, at my husband's stock photography shoot.

Ron and I at our first trade show in Los Angeles where our Easy Daysies booth was sponsored by Radio Disney! How cool was that! (And we outsold Lego!)

Here is the kitchen table where Easy Daysies was born. We still eat and work off this wonderful table. If this table could talk, it would write a book.

Chapter Four:

Principle #4 - Be a Storyteller

Empowerment Quote:

"If you have knowledge, let others light their candles in it."

- *Margaret Fuller*

What does this mean to you and what are you going to do about it?

This was the day. My little family and I were invited to fly out to Toronto to pitch Easy Daysies to five savvy investors on the popular CBC television entrepreneur show called *Dragons' Den* (in the USA, this show's counterpart is *Shark Tank*). My children were two, four, and just turning eight years old. When we got the phone call inviting us, the lovely producer said, "Bring the kids!" I told her how young they were and she replied, "Bring the kids! It's a TV show, not a boardroom!"

"Oh dear," I thought. We brought my mom and dad with us to help with the kids in the green room. Also, knowing that my mom would be there praying for us in the next room was a good thing, too!

Not only were our children young but our entire family had bronchitis, except for my 8-year-old. Every time I practiced speaking, I would cough. A hacking chest cough and raspy voice was not going to stop us though.

Our TV taping time was fixed at 6:30AM Eastern Standard Time. We were scheduled as the second pitch to be filmed. We flew in a day before and knew that the time change would affect our children. This meant that we were actually going to be pitching at 3:30AM Pacific Standard Time, our time.

You can watch our pitch here:

http://www.cbc.ca/dragonsden/pitches/easy-daysies

You will see that our children are all in their pajamas... because it was 3:30AM for their tired, little bodies!

As soon as we arrived at the CBC studios, just before 5:30AM, they gave us a tour and had me display my products on a practice table so that they could examine the product to see if it was television worthy. The team of producers said my plastic boxes were too shiny and that I could not use them.

Panic.

I needed them! How could we go on and pitch without product? I thought quickly and asked if one of the crew could get me some clear tape. I only had minutes but I opened all the boxes and took out the folded paper inserts and taped them to the outside of the boxes. The producers walked by and I quickly showed them my revised products and got their approval. Hallelujah!

Then, all of a sudden, right before going into the green room, my youngest threw up all over the floor. Darn bronchitis. The crew all stepped back as though we brought in a pooping elephant. I went into mommy mode, got down on my hands and knees and wiped it all up. I stood up and said, "It can only get better from here!" Then off to the green room we went. We loved our producers. They gave us last minute tips, and played and drew pictures with our kids. And then we were scooted out to the back stage of the studio. Now, it was my turn to feel nauseous, and it was nerves, not bronchitis.

If you have ever seen this TV show, there is a staircase you have to climb up and then walk along a bridge, and then a metal staircase you have to climb down to get into "the Den." The show is filmed in one take. There are no "Take Twos" or "Take Threes." Just one.

As we waited at the bottom of the stairs, my husband, my rock and anchor, was calm and collected and my kids were young and adorable. Apparently, I was the only one who felt nervous about pitching to five brilliant entrepreneurs who could tear me and our product into tiny pieces and set us on fire. I remember telling my children, "Now, keep your hands to your sides, smile, and don't touch anything! Don't touch your face, don't pick your noses, please don't touch anything!"

My husband held our youngest, and I held my four-and-a-half-year-old son's hand. The crew member gave us the go ahead to walk up the stairs and she told us to wait at the top where there would be another crew member to greet us. As we walked up the metal stairs my stomach got tighter and tighter.

I felt my son squeeze my hand. I looked down at his face, and he said to me with a big smile, "Mommy, I am not scared of Dragons!" I am sure I said something in agreement with him, even though my insides wanted to erupt like a volcano. We got to the top and the next friendly crew member told us to wait and he would count down from ten to zero, and at zero the cameras would be rolling and we were to start walking across the bridge.

There would be no turning back. Some of my thoughts were, "Dear God, please help us not to trip and be the first family on this TV show to all fall down the stairs!" "Please God, help me not to cough when I am presenting." "Oh my goodness! What are we doing here?!"

We got to the bottom of the staircase. There they were, five incredible, multimillionaire geniuses: Jim Treliving, Kevin O'Leary, Arlene Dickenson, Bruce Croxon, and Robert Herjavic. My husband and I have huge respect for all of them because each of them has an incredible story of their own struggle and personal journey to accomplishment. Each of them were self-made success stories. They knew what it was like to be in the trenches, falling on your face and picking yourself up again and again, and moving forward to success. They all understood what it was like to be me. I knew I just had to help them remember.

Stories are Captivating

The most important tool you have to distinguish yourself from others is your story. Your story is what makes you stand out, what connects you, and your offering, to others. A story has the power to take the listener through an emotional journey that can lead them to believe in you and your passion and result in them being invested in you, or becoming your customer or client.

People do not buy what you are selling, they buy *why* you are selling. People buy people.

According to a *Forbes* article ("Sales 101: Sell Stories, Not Products", 2015), "The best sales teams are masters in storytelling." People do not want to be sold *at*, but they do want to connect with you and then make their own informed decision. Is this not what makes a show like *Dragons' Den* or *Shark Tank* the popular investor shows they are?

Back to the *Dragons' Den*. We were told that being invited to the taping of the show does not guarantee that your pitch will air. Even if you get a deal but your pitch is boring, it will not air. It has to be TV-worthy and entertaining.

What makes a great pitch worthy of airing is when the ones pitching are able to captivate us with their own great stories. *Dragons' Den* (and *Shark Tank*) is amazing; it is educational, inspiring, entertaining, and it can be sad too. It is all these things because it is about real people.

Real people share stories of experiences that inspire us, shock us, and that we can relate to. These realities captivate us, move us, anger us, motivate us, and draw us in to want to hear and know more. That is why there are update specials and follow-up stories on *Dragons' Den*, because people want to know more about the stories they have connected with.

We were so honored that we were invited to film three more updates that aired over different seasons. Ford Motor Company was one of the show's sponsors one season and they selected Easy Daysies as one of the nine companies that exemplified their four pillars of success. BDC (Business Development Bank of Canada) chose Easy Daysies as a success story as well, and then we had an update about making dreams come true when we shared about our licensing deal which I had hoped for in our original pitch! It was also exciting to be named one of *Dragons' Den* Top Five Most Heartwarming Pitches as part of the ten-year anniversary of the show. We were told that we had captivated hearts nation-wide. It has been a great honor to work with and learn from Jim, Kevin, Rowan, Alex, and Brad.

Storytelling Begins with Knowing Your Audience and Being Authentically You

Before we were even invited to pitch on *Dragons' Den*, we started our research on each of the investors. We knew their stories, their strengths, their weaknesses, and I even looked up their hobbies since I was going to personalize a magnet for each of their Easy Daysies visual daily schedules.

I needed to know them so I could share my story with them in a relatable and sincere way. No matter what, I had to be me. I could not be anything but me because if they were to partner with me, *me* is what they were going to get. In any sales partnership, there needs to be transparency. Honesty should be spotted right away in sales. If you do not see it or you have to look for it, run the other way.

We were told we would have anywhere between five minutes to forty-five minutes in front of the Dragons. We were with them for 48 incredible minutes. When you watch the episode, you will see the edited version of just over nine exciting, nail biting minutes! What happened was a crazy and unexpected blessing. Our little family incited a bidding war between all five investors! We had the honor of securing two of them to be our partners. Later, one of them shared with us that he invested in us because of who we were. It was crazy. I felt like we knew who they were, too. Know your audience.

As a school teacher, a mom, and as the leader of the Canadian Mompreneurs® represented in British Columbia, I have witnessed failed storytelling attempts as well. The sole reason for failed storytelling is because the speakers do not know their audience. They share stories that are not relatable to the listeners.

I love telling stories and listening to a good story. As a school teacher, I loved watching the faces of my captive audience of children as they would listen to me with wide eyes and unflinching mouths, as no one dared make a sound to interrupt. I also noticed when we had guest speakers who did not captivate the audience, whether it was a room full of children or women entrepreneurs. Have enough respect for yourself and your client to know them. Do not waste their precious time, because if you do, you will definitely not see any of their precious money.

Stories are Memorable

People remember stories because stories evoke emotion and, even though we may not remember who told us the story, we will always remember how the story made us feel. A story told well gets the listener to relate and connect to what you are saying. Powerful emotions are awoken and imprinted in their hearts and minds. According to Jerome

Bruner's book, *Actual Minds, Possible Worlds* (Harvard University Press), stories are remembered up to twenty-two times more than facts and figures alone.

Best of all, a good story gets shared. Who doesn't like to tell or listen to a good story? So, what is your story?

What is your passion, your why?

How did you arrive at this passionate state that has caused you to offer what you sell? Remember, it is not about the makeup you offer, or the real estate you sell, or the coaching you do. It is about how what you offer is simply an extension of your passion. Help your prospective customer know you first—share your story. The secret to this principle is that your story is what they will remember and what they will share with others. Then, the sales will follow.

A good story is powerful. It takes the listener on an emotional journey of where they have been, or where they currently are, to where they want to be. If they can connect with the positive feeling of where they want to be and realize that they can get that with what you are offering, they will want what you have.

Here is one more fun fact about storytelling: Author and speaker Paul Zak shares in the *Harvard Review* that listening to stories causes our brains to release oxytocin, a signal in the brain that says it is safe to approach others. This hormone is produced when we are shown kindness or trust and prompts cooperation with others. This makes me think about how we as parents use story time to *sell* bedtime to our children and get them to cooperate. The selling power of storytelling must be true.

Action Strategy #4: Be a Story Teller.
Think about your businesses and write down:
1. How will you apply this principle to your business?
2. What is the promise you want to achieve with this strategy?
3. What is the measurable result you want, with a date of accomplishment?
4. Share this action strategy and all three parts above with the person you chose to hold you accountable in the introduction of this book.

Chapter Five:
Principle #5 – Be a Connector

Empowerment Quote:

"Successful people are always looking for opportunities to help others. Unsuccessful people are always asking, What's in it for me?"

- Brian Tracy

What does this mean to you and what are you going to do about it?

As mentioned, one of my favorite quotes comes from Maya Angelou who eloquently said, *"Success is liking who you are, liking what you do, and liking how you do it."* At the end of the day, if you do not like who you are, it does not matter how much money you make or who you know. Success to me is living a life worthy of being copied by my children.

I believe that in order to sell well you have to be a great connector. You have to believe that there is greater good in working for the betterment of others, to connect people with those who can truly assist their journey when you are unable, that we are stronger together than alone.

Being a connector is fundamental in the longevity of your relationship with your customer or future customer. To be the best connector comprises two parts:

A) How you connect with your customer.
B) How you connect your customer with others who can improve their journey.

Connecting with Your Customer

Connecting with our customers begins with knowing them. What do they like? What do they buy? Where do they live? Where do they work? Where do they go on vacation? What is their educational status? Where do they go to relax? What shows do they watch? What social media platforms do they frequent? Do they like finding deals or do they prefer paying for high priced items?

If you are selling to another company, you also need to show them that you understand who they are, their mission statement, their target market, and so on. Get to know the company as though it were a person.

The best connection happens when three principles are achieved. First, know your number one target market. Second, make active listening a priority. Third, understand that the way you connect others speaks of who you are, not what you sell.

1. Know the Number One Target Market

Let us focus right now on how to connect with the number one shopper in the household: the woman. I am often invited on stages and panels to share about how to market to moms, from the Marketing to Moms Conference in New York, to the Canadian Health Food Association in Vancouver.

Moms know best. Let's take that and run with it! Why is it important to market to moms, and how do we do it successfully? First, women control $12 trillion of the overall $18.4 trillion in global consumer spending; that is, two thirds of the world's spending power. Secondly, women make over 80% of the purchasing decisions in households across North America. Thirdly, moms make purchasing decisions not only for themselves but for their children, their spouses, their homes and their gifts to others.

Moms are influencers and they are constantly sharing their favorite and least favorite finds on social media. So, if a brand or business can earn the attention of a mom, they have hit an incredible marketing gold mine!

The question then is, how do we gain the attention of a mom?

I believe that the three best ways are as follows:

1. Grab their attention with empowerment. A great example is the Swagger Wagon, which shows you a cool rapping mom in her Toyota Sienna. Another great slogan is Staples' "Make More Happen" to instigate ideas! (In one of my blog posts at www.easydaysies.com, I share how this was personally true for me in starting my own business, Easy Daysies®, with Staples as part of my story!) Studies show that women are more interested in information that puts them in control, whereas men are more interested in information that helps them beat the system.
2. Strike an emotional chord. Show women that you understand what is important to them, like family time, parenthood, and kids growing up too fast. Show them that you understand the challenges of being a mom.
3. Be short, sweet, and sharable. Think of a 140-character tweet and say it simply and impactfully. Moms are super busy, so be efficient and honor their time. Make sure what you are sharing is meaningful and useful so it is worthy of sharing.

Lastly, be on the social media platforms they are on, like (at the time of this writing) Facebook. Moms are on Facebook all the time. All types of moms are there: soon to be moms, moms on maternity leave, moms of six kids, work-at-home moms, and even grand-moms.

Moms are on social media to look for ideas, solutions and tips, to maintain relationships, and to avoid isolation. Moms congregate and share opinions. They love telling you what they think, so communicate with them and ask them what they think! They want to let you know how to help them and their families have easier, happier, more affordable lives. Moms spend much of their time on social media sharing and consuming information about brands and products, so give them something worthy of sharing! The saying "Mom knows best" has a lot of weight, so connect with them and get these moms talking about your brand to their friends and family for you.

2. Make Active Listening A Priority

When a client or potential client connects with you and you find that you are actively listening, you will hear other areas of need or wants they may have. Active listening is hearing what your client is saying and then taking time to repeat back what you are hearing so that they feel heard and understood. It is also a good opportunity for you to clarify what their true needs are. Take this opportunity to get to really know your client and make helpful connections for them.

Let's say you are selling makeup or offering business coaching and you hear your client share that she is seeking a good insurance company or planning on taking a vacation soon. Here is when you can deeply connect with them and show that you have all their interests at heart. When you share with them that you know of another person who could help them with their insurance needs, vacation planning, or car engine problems, and you connect them to someone you trust, you will make them feel listened to and valued.

Connecting Your Customer with Others

3. The Way You Connect Others Speaks of Who You Are, Not What You Sell

At the same time, your referral can also help a client, friend, or potential customer whom you know, who is a great insurance broker, or a travel agent who is starting out in their own business, or a local business you fully support. This goes back to my belief that we are stronger together. These individuals will truly appreciate the referral as well. People helping people makes the world go round. Help with no strings attached, with no expectation that they should be referring you back. Having such an expectation removes all the sincerity and purpose of the initial act. Honesty, sincerity, and integrity cannot be bought or sold, they are pretty much irreplaceable. So, guard yours in all you do and say. Be sure of who you refer because their core values reflect as your own.

Action Strategy #5: Be a Connector

Think about your businesses and write down:

1. How will you apply this principle to your business?

2. What is the promise you want to achieve with this strategy?

3. What is the measurable result you want, with a date of accomplishment?

4. Share this action strategy and all three parts above with the person you chose to hold you accountable in the introduction of this book.

SELL YOUR PASSION

Chapter Six:
Principle #6 – Be Innovative

Empowerment Quote:

Innovation distinguishes between a leader and a follower.

— Steve Jobs, Founder of Apple Corporation

What does this mean to you and what are you going to do about it?

Passion means being innovative, adapting and changing as necessary to be one step ahead to meet the needs of your customers. To provide what they need, even before they ask for it. The passion behind Easy Daysies causes me to actively listen to my customers and to be innovative and create products and solutions for their changing needs. Passion cannot sit still. It is continuously at work.

Innovation is described as a new method, idea, or product. In this vein, people tend to think of products, particularly technology such as computers and smart phones. But just as often, innovations in the way we do things (for example, PayPal was a new way to collect funds, and iTunes was a new way to consume music), or products that made things better or easier (the Internet, automobiles, and the telegram), were all ideas that led to plenty of other innovations. That is, you don't need to create a brand new product to be innovative, you just need to find something that people either want or need, and then provide it!

In the case of Easy Daysies, it was a new product (magnetic daily schedules for children), using an established method (the "shape of the day" I always provided in my classroom), based on a new idea (if it works for 30 children in a classroom, it should work for one child at home). But as you will see later, I have been innovating off that first idea for years as I listen to my customers and respond to their needs.

When you have a good understanding of how your service or product is simply an extension of your passion, you will have people asking you for it and wanting to tell others about it for you. People love sharing great finds.

Easy Daysies has made me a more complete person. It has allowed me to share my passion and put it to good use, to be that outlet that only it could be. Now I am honored to speak about my passion to large audiences of entrepreneurs, educators, parents, to aspiring entrepreneurs, and sometimes to small groups of school-aged students. It is all about being innovative enough to see a need and then provide an answer to that need.

Easy Daysies was created with the goal of helping children have easier days and I am truly blessed and honored to have created something that is helping to improve the quality of life for children and families, as well as both children and adults with special needs.

What has kept me working at the kitchen table until 3 or 4AM were the e-mails and messages I received from families and health care providers. Parents kindly took the time to share how their child with autism, or their non-verbal developmentally delayed child, or their child with ADHD or anxiety, or their foster children, were succeeding in their day because of Easy Daysies.

My heart melts with appreciation and humility as I read that a mom with three children, all with autism and under the age of seven, is so happy because Easy Daysies helps her to not have to "talk talk talk" all day long anymore because of the visual communication Easy Daysies provides for their family.

When I read an e-mail from a foster parent sharing that Easy Daysies has taken away the anxiety and insecurity in their home because their kids can see and know what is happening when life is so unpredictable for them, I know Easy Daysies is making a real difference. When I see an e-mail from a mom pregnant with her fourth child say that her husband has made her write to inform me that they cannot believe their children have stopped arguing in the mornings and that the whole family now sleeps twenty minutes more each morning because of Easy Daysies, I know that Easy Daysies is working.

When a parent writes to share that "Easy Daysies significantly improves the quality of *Emma's* life" (their daughter who is non-verbal with low-functioning autism) because she now has the ability to communicate by using Easy Daysies as *her words*, I am humbled and believe that Easy Daysies is making an impact.

The passion that flows through Easy Daysies is continuously recognized. Jim Treliving even stated that my passion caused him to love magnets (my products are magnetic daily schedules).

With the product helping so many people, no need to innovate, right? Wrong. One of the most important lessons in sales is to always listen to your customers, so you know what they like and don't like, and use that feedback to give them what they want. Mastering innovation is giving them what they need.

I received so many e-mails and messages from families over the last few years about how they were not only using Easy Daysies for their young children, but were also buying them for their adult family members with early memory loss issues, like Alzheimer's and dementia. So, once again, I did the research and discovered that there was not a product like Easy Daysies for adults. After seven focus groups, research, and development, the adult version of Easy Daysies was born through a series called "My Day" by Easy Daysies®.

Innovation is the secret sauce for the survival, growth, and value of any business. It is what will keep customers buying from you and seeking you out as a leader in your industry. Innovation results from observing the changing demands and needs of your customer base, combined with the ambition you have to move ahead of your competitors.

Whether you sell a product or a service, you want to let your customers know that you are always doing your best to serve them and meet their needs. Innovation is not just about the invention of something new, it is also about updating the way you do business to complement your changing marketplace. Being innovative is about seeing, responding, and solving problems.

It is about being customer-centric. Customers see value from companies who understand their needs and deliver products and services that support their lifestyles. The customer wants us to empathize with them, to feel their pain, and when we can genuinely demonstrate that understanding, they buy and become loyal patrons. Do you know what solidifies them as loyal patrons? It is ensuring that they feel they are in control. This is when they feel that the product or service was made for them and that they chose it rather than it being sold to them.

The Innovation Begins

When I first created Easy Daysies, it was done out of parent demand in my classrooms. I made them off my kitchen table for the parents who asked me to make something similar to what I had in the front of my classroom to help their children cooperate better at home, to become more independent, to just literally get out the door faster in the morning.

I did not just rush out and make it into a product; I did the research. I found that one in four school age children has anxiety issues, one in six has learning disabilities, one in 48 has autism spectrum disorder (and the list goes on), there is a desperate need for tools to help our children succeed. I listened to what the families wanted.

Actually, I listened for eight years. It wasn't until I was pregnant with our third child that I thought about working from home, and thought there might be a product idea there.

I knew there was a need since parents had been asking me to make these for years. I knew that studies showed that children as young as preschool age benefit from visual schedules because they cooperate better and become more confident, all because they can see and predict what is happening next. My research showed that there was no other product out there that is a magnetic daily visual schedule for children who need help with prompting memory and assisting with smoother event transitions.

I looked at how to make this product as a solution for others and found out it would cost $1400 to make my first batch of product. So, I saved up by doing extra tutoring and selling crafts at craft fairs. This product was going to help busy families and children have easier days, so that is how it got the name "Easy Daysies."

I launched Easy Daysies two days after our third baby was born (she came early). It sold out in one month. Easy Daysies then somehow started getting online reviews based on our website, and soon became the #1 Back to School Must Have in *Parents Canada* magazine. Stores started to call asking if they could carry my product. Soon Easy Daysies was in two stores, then 26 stores, and then 67 stores. Easy Daysies was available in 1500 stores across North America in the first four years. It was much easier to sell an innovative product to prospective retailers than just another "me too" product.

I bought the provisional patent for magnetic daily visual schedules in 2011 to protect our creation when we first released it.

We are proud to be making products that help children, families, and individuals improve the quality of their lives. There are many planners and calendars in the marketplace, but this was the first magnetic visual daily schedule. The key observation in my research was that children don't think abstractly like adults do (adults look at today, next week, next month, etc.), but they tend to think about two things: what I'm doing now, and what I'm doing next.

I Listened to Teachers

I started getting e-mails and Facebook messages from teachers asking where the classroom version of Easy Daysies was. So, the classroom version was born! This was an interesting development. Easy Daysies started out as an idea to take classroom ideas into the home, then came back to the classroom as an innovation in creating the "shape of the day." Most teachers, myself included, created their own classroom schedules with construction paper, clip art, felt pens, lamination, and velcro. There were some commercial products, but they were flimsy and did not have pictures for non-readers. So our innovation was to create sturdy, magnetic classroom schedules with large illustrations.

We created visual daily schedules that are a necessary classroom management tool for teachers and an easy-to-use visual tool for parents to support children by lessening anxiety and creating confident, cooperative, and independent children. Child psychologists, healthcare providers, and educators recommend Easy Daysies by name to families who are too busy and lack the ability to make their own visual schedules.

Many child psychologists, healthcare providers, and educators recommend families make their own visual schedules, however families are either too busy or lack the know-how to make them. Parents, educators, and health professionals are thrilled when they stumble upon Easy Daysies and discover that they already exist and are so affordable!

Innovation Has No Limits

When I created the first version of my product, it was just a pack of task magnets. I listened to how families were using these magnets on their fridges and when they had to go to grandma's house, they would have to take the individual magnets off their fridge, put them in a Ziplock bag and then rebuild the schedule once they got there. So, I created a portable fold & go board for the magnets to be placed on.

I listened to how some families with special needs children were excited to have Easy Daysies and would take the magnet task that was just completed and move it from the front of the fridge to the side on the fridge to make a clear distinction that the task was done. So, when I created the fold & go board, I added a "To Do" column and a "Done" column so that the child could move the magnet and have a clear distinction that the task was completed. In my research, I also discovered that the kinesthetic move from picking up the magnet and moving it from the "To Do" to the "Done" side is like getting a pat on the back for the child, similar to how we feel when we cross off a "to do" list.

I researched that a certain colour of blue was most soothing to children with anxiety and we use that colour on all our magnets. Oh yes, I also made the board a certain length to help parents understand that you only want to list no more than six or seven tasks so as to not overwhelm the child. The length of the board is for the parent to understand that you want to help your child become successful and independent at a specific routine, such as at morning or bedtime.

I tell people that in the startup phase there are two questions you want to ask yourself when starting a business, when you think you have the next big idea. First, does it already exist? Most great ideas are already created, so if you do the research and see that it already exists, no problem—see how you can make it better. Second, ask yourself if your product or service solves an existing problem. If you can answer "yes" to this question, you are on the right track.

Innovation is Born from Demand.

Easy Daysies was created off my kitchen table by parent demand when I was a school teacher. As mentioned, over the years many families shared that they were buying our daily visual schedules not just for their young children, but also for their adult family members with early memory loss due to dementia or Alzheimer's, or for adult children with brain injury or special needs. I have done the research and discovered that the only products out there for adults with memory loss issues are repurposed toys and children's puzzles. I believe that no adult would find much dignity in using children's toys.

We felt that these individuals deserved an adult version of Easy Daysies, so I spent almost two years meeting with focus groups made up of health care providers who work with adults with memory loss, and visiting seniors' residences to create a product they like and that would help them have happier, more successful days.

Our new line is created to help adults (and young adults) with memory loss issues, special needs, brain injury, dementia, or Alzheimer's have more autonomy and more independent, confident, and successful days with the visual reminding of "My Day" by Easy Daysies.

It is staggering to know that every 66 seconds in the USA someone is diagnosed with dementia. In Canada, more than 25,000 individuals are diagnosed with Alzheimer's disease every year. Easy Daysies wants to provide a simple tool to make days easier for these people.

In order to create the adult version, we asked focus groups specific questions over two years. After seven focus groups, "My Day" by Easy Daysies® for Adults was created with applicable visual reminders (e.g. Take Medication, Turn Off Stove, Appointments, Pay Bills, etc.) to make each day easier! And there is no product out there like Easy Daysies® Daily Visual Schedules.

Innovation Begins with How You Do Business

Wallis Evera, a gorgeous women's clothing line made with natural and sustainable materials, quoted me on their website when they asked for a word of advice for women in business. I shared, "The future is full of potential—make sure to approach it with boldness and kindness." Listen to your market and ask them what they want; the future is full of potential. It is as simple as going on Facebook or Instagram and putting the right questions out there. Be simple and clear on what you are asking so you get well-defined answers that will help you help your customers.

Remember, innovation does not mean just creating new products and services, but also changing the way you do things. Perhaps what needs to change is the way you are talking to your audience, or where you are talking to them, or perhaps it is the method by which you are presenting your offering. For example, people love sharing great videos. So, you may want to start a YouTube channel or Facebook Live.

When you are innovative, others want to talk about you and what you have to offer. I get excited when I see people share on social media how our products have helped their families. It lets me know that our products are doing what they are supposed to be doing.

It is always a privilege when others recognize our innovations. We were honored when the Chamber of Commerce awarded Easy Daysies with the Excellence in Business Award in 2014, and when Ford Company selected Easy Daysies as one of nine companies exemplifying Ford's Four Pillars of Success and was recognized in particular for innovation, and in 2018 when Easy Daysies was named one of the Top Ten Most Innovative Small Businesses in British Columbia. Easy Daysies continues to be recognized for our product development and has won twelve national and international awards to date.

But it is not awards and accolades that help me work late into the night. Rather, it is the messages I mentioned earlier in this chapter, from grateful families whose lives are changed for the better.

What am I trying to say here? Be innovative. Keep solving the problems your customers are facing.

The greatest affirmation that the passion and innovation behind Easy Daysies was indeed on the right path was that our products were recommended by child psychologists, occupational therapists, behaviour interventionists, and speech and language pathologists.

Easy Daysies is being recommended for families with children and adults who have a wide range of health, medical, and learning issues, such as autism spectrum disorder, anxiety, anyone who is non-verbal or developmentally delayed, attention deficit disorder and ADHD, as well as memory loss conditions such as Alzheimer's and dementia.

Being innovative requires us to know not just what our customers currently want and need, but also what they *will* want and *will* need. You want to be the first one to be able to offer them a solution to their problem. When you can do this, your customers cannot help but sell for you. They will gladly share about your offerings to their friends and families because you are a leader in your field and you have an answer to their need.

Action Strategy #6: Be Innovative.

Think about your businesses and write down:

1. How will you apply this principle to your business?

2. What is the promise you want to achieve with this strategy?

3. What is the measurable result you want, with a date of accomplishment?

4. Share this action strategy and all three parts above with the person you chose to hold you accountable in the introduction of this book.

Chapter Seven:
Principle #7 - Be Contagious

Empowerment Quote:

"Knowledge is power, but enthusiasm pulls the switch."

- Ivern Ball

What does this mean to you and what are you going to do about it?

It would be a dream for our phones to be ringing off the hook and e-mails to be flooding our inbox with orders and appointment requests for our product or service. This can be a reality. How do we create a frenzy and get people talking about our offering? How do we spread the word about our offering so that others will not only want it but can't help spreading the word for us? How do we get an impact like we did when we aired that first time on Dragons' Den when we saw orders pouring in across the country and saw that at one point we were getting twelve new hits on our website per second! Just imagine you are doing something other than selling—perhaps taking a trip with your family, reading a book, or trying out a new restaurant with friends—all without a care about work or making money. How is this possible? It *is* possible because your passion has become contagious, and while you are enjoying life, others are selling your services or products *for* you. Wouldn't that be great?

As Ivern Ball says, *"Knowledge is power, but enthusiasm pulls the switch."* Contained knowledge is great but useless, unless it can be released in a way to benefit others. When you have something great to share, it should be released like fireworks—enthusiastically! And when it's your passion you are sharing about, it is exciting every time, not belaboring.

When we are clear on our passion, we should be running around like we are on fire. We should be easily sharing about our passion, letting that fire catch around us, and watching it catch from others. If your product or service is something that could help someone, others will want to know and share about it. When your passion catches on, people are going to share about it without you having to do anything at all. That is called contagious marketing, which converts into sales. I am just skimming the surface here, as there is a lot more that goes into making sure that your business is set up for sales to happen (e.g. clear and available marketing tools, an efficient website, etc.).

In my entrepreneurial journey and through mentoring and coming alongside some incredible women entrepreneurs, I have had the honor of witnessing some incredibly creative methods of contagious selling. Contagious selling is about developing relationships, building trust, and most of all it is about sharing the desire to make a positive difference in the lives of others. People love sharing great finds that help other people. Why not do your part to make your own product or service contagious?

Someone once told me, "If you believe that your product benefits others, how dare you keep it to yourself?"

How dare you?

If you believe that you have something incredible to offer others, why are you not running around talking about it? If you have something that can help someone save money, live longer, feel stronger, or be more confident, safe, or happy, would you not want to eagerly tell them about it as soon as possible?

Notice I am talking about "sharing," not selling. When you share with honest excitement, other people will want to share that same honest excitement with you and for you, because they believe in you. When you are sharing (not selling) the best secret ever (the benefits of your offering) people can't help but listen and pass it on.

We so easily "share" about the great finds we discover. We Tweet, Instagram or Facebook a photo of the best ever savoury spiral potato on a stick we have ever eaten, telling everyone we know that they just have to head on over to XYZ food truck to buy one because they are so good! But sometimes we neglect to do this for our own business. We need to share that same excitement about our own products and services so that we can help others discover the great things we have to offer.

Word of mouth "sharing" is the original and most successful method of contagious selling. We all know this but seem to forget that this easy, powerful, and free practice begins with us, the business owner, sales representative, consultant, or entrepreneur.

I have a very smart friend who enthusiastically shares about her hair products. Her name is also Elaine, and this dynamo of a woman makes it look easy, but know that she has trained and worked super hard to make it look effortless.

She knows that her hair products are not for everyone, as it is an expensive product line, so she will excitedly share about its benefits with others and ask them if they happen to know anyone who may be interested in a product that helps with hair re-growth for those experiencing hair loss.

Her method is brilliant. In asking for the referral, her enthusiasm combined with sharing the benefits of the products, draws the interest of the listener, who will then often say, "Yes, I know someone who needs it—I do!" Her technique is smart because she is not selling directly to the potential customer, and as such they do not feel "sold at" and she is also able to educate the listener about the benefits of her product so they can spread the word for her. This lady creates a contagious conversation around her wherever she goes!

Another wonderful friend of mine, Petra, sells food seasonings, spices, and cooking gadgets. She creatively found a way to demonstrate her products, while getting paid to do it. Petra teaches cooking classes for children using her products on Saturday mornings and on teacher professional development days when parents are seeking activities to occupy their children. She also has a back end where families get to shop at a discount to order the same cooking gadgets and spices and seasonings that were just used in the class so that the children can repeat the recipe at home. Brilliant! Everyone loves her cooking classes and not only leave asking when the next one is, but is also spreading the word.

Jacqueline is another brilliant, contagious seller who knows how to get people talking and sharing about her business, Homeworks Etc. She owns a brick and mortar location where people can come in and make a DIY project they can decorate their home with or give to a deserving friend. Her venue is gorgeous and can host small meetings, birthday events, and staff parties. What is "magic" is how everyone shares photos of their incredible projects they create on Instagram and Facebook, telling their friends and family that they too can make their own DIY project at this awesome venue. Believe me, it works, I have been there several times already and have posted my own photos bragging about her business and sending others there.

Here is a look at what I have learned in my years of selling from off my kitchen table that has led to my product line selling over seven figures in gross sales.

Seven Steps to Contagious Sales

1. Know your Product or Service Inside Out

First and foremost, you must believe in what you are offering. Like I said in an earlier chapter, your product or service should simply be an extension of your passion, your desire to provide a specific solution to a specific problem. You have something that can help someone else. This should be so exciting to you. If you are not convinced by your own offering, your customers will see right through you and you can forget about any sale.

If you do not love it, or see its value and importance, no one else will either. If you cannot sell it to yourself, you will not be able to sell it at all. When you believe in your product you will have confidence to sell it naturally and effortlessly. Others will want it because of your sincere belief in it, and your confidence and passion for it!

Business Insider interviewed Kevin O'Leary on his top five sales tips and this is what he had to say:

"You have to love the product you're selling," he said. "You have to have an emotional bond to it. It has to be oozing from every pore: This is the greatest product you have ever sold."

If you get a chance to watch our original pitch on Dragons' Den you will hear Kevin O'Leary say to me that my enthusiasm for my product was "oozing out of me." Perhaps that is what persuaded him to invest in Easy Daysies and cause all five investors to fight over it.

2. Know your Customer Inside Out

Learn about your customers. Listen to them. No matter what you say or how well you dress or how funny you are, your customer will not trust you until they believe that you hear them. We need to listen to what the customer or client needs and wants.

Take time to know your customer, ask them questions to help them figure out what it is they truly want. Be honest and up-front, and if you don't know an answer, tell them that you will find it for them. People buy *people* more than products or services, especially offline. When a trusting relationship is established, sales will happen.

Knowing and understanding your customer allows you to help them better. The best way to appeal to a woman's attention is with empowerment. Studies show that women are more interested in information that puts them in control, whereas men are more interested in information that helps them beat the system.

I quickly learned that the power behind reaching my market was getting influencers to know, understand, and love my product. For me, my influencers were three-fold: moms, special education specialists, and health-care providers (such as occupational therapists, child psychologists, and speech and language pathologists).

Easy Daysies was being referred to at health, educational, parenting, and toy seminars. I did not have to say a word because Easy Daysies was being shared about at workshops by healthcare specialists, counselors, social workers and other professionals as they used Easy Daysies to educate people about how to use visual aids for persons dealing with communication and anxiety challenges. This was incredible. I would see child psychologists and parenting experts share about Easy Daysies in parenting magazines, in their books, in *Huffington Post* articles, on television programs, and on stages across North America. There is nothing more contagious in selling than the word being spread by a trusted influencer.

3. Create a Sense of Urgency and Scarcity

Limit the time or offer. People know if they want your product or service almost as soon as you ask, and this will help them make a quicker decision and not procrastinate and forget about you. This is why Facebook, Instagram contests, and e-mail blasts with one day sale offers do so well.

4. Dedicate Time Daily to Sales. This could mean connecting with old and new prospects.

It is very easy to spend all our time on doing everything else but prospecting. If you don't schedule it and hold yourself accountable, you won't do it. Not because you don't want to, but because you will not get to it. Start by dedicating two hours each morning to income generating activities and watch your business grow.

5. Follow Up and Follow Through

Always follow through with doing what you say you are going to do. This not only helps build a trusting relationship but shows integrity and perseverance. Be short and to the point and respect people's time. Your customers will feel remembered—special even—when you take the time to follow up. I have heard over and over that it can take up to seven follow ups before a sale happens!

6. Build Relationships By Being Real

Always be honest always with who you are and what you represent. If you work from home, don't be afraid or embarrassed to share that you are a small home-based business. I have found that companies and people I work with and sell to appreciate that I am a small business, that I work off my kitchen table. They give me breaks that they would not give if they were dealing with a larger company.

I have been very grateful for this kindness.

Personalize the way you do things. You will be remembered and stand out from your competition. When I was the one delivering orders to my independent retailers I use to bring homemade chocolate chip cookies. Kevin O'Leary pokes fun at me in his book, *Cold Hard Truth on Family, Kids and Money*, saying that I am on the right track, even though you would never see him bringing fresh baked cookies into a business meeting (page 216). He applauds me for being me and personalizing my relationships with my clients which, in his words, "add a tremendous amount of equity in perpetuity." He says people will want to buy your product or service because they trust you. It is about building lasting relationships.

Let your customer get to know you. Learn to humbly share about yourself. If you and your offerings have won awards or appeared in media, share them! What was your biggest success last month? Share your achievements. Someone will appreciate what you shared and tell others for you! That could lead to sales or more media exposure, you just never know. But if you keep your product, service, solution, and your successes to yourself, you may as well close shop right now.

7. Find Your Niche

Your product or service is not for everyone. Once you've established who your product or service is for, serve them well. You will not only stand out, but the word will spread about you and your offerings in the circles you want them to. The most effective and contagious way to sell is to focus your energy on your target market.

* * *

The impact of Easy Daysies has been humbling. I never thought I would be an entrepreneur or an inventor of educational products that would help alleviate anxiety and improve a person's quality of life. I did know that helping and serving others was what I was born to do, and that is the passion that fuels Easy Daysies. This is how Easy Daysies is an extension of my passion.

It is this passion that is driven by the impact Easy Daysies has in the lives of its users. The testimonials I receive from families continues to fuel me when I feel like I am hanging on by a thread, working many late nights in a row and up again for 6AM conference calls, that need to be done before my three children wake up. In these past years, my passion has continued to grow and grow.

My passion has caused me to challenge myself beyond what I thought I could do. On my podcast, I share about pitching a product I created off my kitchen table to my first local retailer, my first national retailer, to five savvy investors on a popular TV show on CBC called *Dragons' Den*, securing Kevin O'Leary and Jim Treliving as partners, to getting multiple licensing deals and distribution, to winning Kevin Harrington's *Pitch Tank*, to becoming one of the Top Five Most Heartwarming Pitches on *Dragons' Den*, to being featured in *Forbes*, *Financial Post*, and countless other media. It all stems from realizing that my product is simply an extension of my passion to help children and individuals have easier and happier days.

Passion pushes you to go for it. Passion pulls you up when you are at your lowest point in your journey. Passion helps you break through glass ceilings created by society or even yourself.

I have learned that it is okay to have a good cry when no one is looking, and also when everyone is looking. I have learned that it is always more important to be true to yourself than to regret a decision later.

I have learned that passion is the fuel that keeps your "sails" and "sales" going.

* * *

Successfully selling our passion means taking the focus off ourselves. It means shifting the energy or spotlight onto the receiver, client or customer. To focus on sharing how our offering solves our customer's problem, rather than focusing on self-doubt or on what we think we cannot do. It means identifying and acknowledging our expertise and sharing it boldly. If we do not know what our uniqueness or specialization is, our customer will not know either. Keep listening to your customers and share how your offering is not only keeping up to their changing needs but is actually a leader in that innovation. Lastly, people buy *people*, not products or services. Be customer-centric, be genuine, be passionate.

Successful selling is just the action of sharing your passion to those who would benefit from it. Because this book is meant to be a quick and easy read on strategies that have worked for me, my seven principles to selling one's passion effortlessly and contagiously, there are just these seven chapters. There is no Conclusion chapter; you create the conclusion. Just you, taking action on any of these principles. So, go for it. I am still standing here, opening the door for you. The next chapter is yours.

Action Strategy #7: Be Contagious.
Think about your businesses and write down:
1. How will you apply this principle to your business?
2. What is the promise you want to achieve with this strategy?
3. What is the measurable result you want, with a date of accomplishment?
4. Share this action strategy and all three parts above with the person you chose to hold you accountable in the introduction of this book.

Acknowledgements

When people ask me how I manage (cope, survive, thrive) running three small businesses, speaking at events across the continent, hosting a podcast, selling at tradeshow after tradeshow, and all that comes with raising three children, I have often joked that it is the result of lots of coffee and chocolate. As much as I do contribute to the global coffee market, my strength and sanity come from my faith. I start each morning breathing in the Word of God and often end it on my knees. Giving my first minutes of my day in gratitude and meditation on scripture fuels me for what the day will bring. It is not easy, but thank God for Bible apps!

I thank God for His awesome grace towards me. I stumble and fall every day, but He picks me up unfailingly. He truly is my strong tower. (Psalm 61:3) He has been by my side and gives me patience and strength when things seem to take longer than I can handle. (2 Timothy 4:17) I have assurance that I can do all things through strength that comes from Him (Philippians 4:13) because He does not give me more than I can bear. (I Corinthians 10:13) I am always so very grateful and blown away because He gives me more than I can even ask for or imagine (Ephesians 3:20) in His perfect time. I have learned to hide this favorite verse in my heart, that I hope to live out each day and exemplify for my children: "Be joyful in hope; patient in affliction, faithful in prayer." (Romans 12:12) I will always count everything as a blessing because I know that all good and perfect gifts come from the Father above.

I am blessed to have the most incredible partner in life, Ron, who truly makes my world spin. He is the sunrise in my every day and the sunset every night. Yes, as corny as it may sound, he still makes my heart flutter when I see him unexpectedly from across the room. He is the perfect balance for me. I am a crazy kite that excitedly goes here and there, and he is the calm, patient man who untangles me from the tree tops. He is the best father to our children. When we met, he promised to make me laugh and cry every day. He is a good promise keeper. He is my best friend, my crush, my mentor, my e-mail proof-reader, my sounding board, my wake-up call, my business partner, and the one I love to have adventures with. I would not be who I am without this man.

I am so grateful for the three angels I am honored and blessed to hear call me Mom. Abigail, Justin, and Naomi are the most loving, patient, caring, empathetic, funny, supportive, bright, and understanding children I have ever met. I was a school teacher for fourteen years, and taught Sunday School for twenty-three, so, I have actually seen and known a lot of children! These kids have lived in a house (or two) filled with boxes and pallets, helped assemble packaging, set up tradeshows, listen to and be a part of speeches, countless interviews, many television shows and news broadcasts, see their mommy off at the airport and then welcome her with home-made "Welcome Home" signs week after week. They have seen their mom fall on her knees and cry and come to her side to pray with her. They have done many happy dances with their mom when prayers get answered. They have taught me to persevere (as a work at home mom) because the true meaning of success is the amount of family time you have rather than the amount of dollars in your bank account. I love you Abigail. I love you Justin. I love you Naomi. You all give the best hugs.

I am grateful for our parents, Andrew and MaryAnn, Marcel and Muriel. You have taught me about love, family, faith, and sacrifice. I love you for trusting and believing in me and Ron. Your support goes beyond all the times you have stepped in to take care of our children so we can fly off to tradeshow after tradeshow. You are who I aspire to be like. Your love and wisdom are the arms that have silently held us together. Thank you with all my heart.

Thank you to my sisters and brothers-in-law, Catherine, Michele, Niki, Rachele, Ashlee, Doug, Rich, and Aaron. You do not know how much your kind words and offers of help have touched my heart and kept me going. I will always remember how you have helped me from taking care of our children, to assisting at product launches, to shipping orders, to words of advice and encouragement. Dear, sweet aunty Catherine who take the kids bowling and pizza regularly, all my sisters(in law) and both moms who would take products home with them to fold or glue or package to make it a lighter load for me, I have not forgotten. Thank you with all my heart.

Thank you to all of you who gave me a chance and believed in Ron and I and Easy Daysies. I am grateful for every word of advice, thank you Jim Treliving, Kevin O'Leary, Rowan Anderson, Brad Hallwood, Alex Kenjeev, Henry Lim, Jason Goto, Maria Locker, Julie Cole, Nancy Parker, Mr. and Mrs. Mack, and Sharon Vinderine. From the very beginning when I just launched, new to the world of manufacturing and distribution, thank you for believing in a product that helps others have easier days, Kirsten Anderson, Henry Lim, Matthew Werrell, Diane Shaw Foo, Scott, Sandra and Patti, Ann Barta, Jimmy Kim and Heather Reisman, Stacey, Chris and Brandi, the ACCO Brands Canada Family, Catherine Ellsmere and Tracie Tighe and Michelle MacMillan of CBC Dragons' Den.

Thank you to all my dear friends who have shown me support from buying my first ever product, to showing up at my door unexpectedly to offer help after sleepless nights. Thank you for the accountability, hugs, laughs, words of wisdom, and support. I am so grateful for you all, Linda, Vanessa and Mitcheal, Gina and Robert, Christy, Sherri, Jen, Judith, Mel, Noula, Tracey, Lorie, Tanya, Tara, Samantha, Arlana, Sandy, Sandra, Shannon, Paula, and Leah. To ladies that hold me accountable, because we are stronger together: Wendy, Maria, Sharon, Kim, Petra, Duette, Jacqueline, Elaine, Lisa, Angela and Yvonne, and so many more. To the women who lift me up in shared prayer and boxes of Kleenex, Carolyn, Kirby, Laura, Jenny, Lilian, Lisa, Courtney, Yvonne, Sharon, Angie, Mandy, Korena, Loretta, and Sindy.

Thank you to Ron Comeau and Laura Kjolby for being the first eyes to read this and edit this book. Thank you to the publisher that wanted to make this book happen and challenged me to do it.

Thank you to all the children and families that I have had the honor of teaching and learning with, whom demanded for me to make my first ever product line. Thank you to the teams of moms who worked and laughed on my kitchen table with me.

It truly does take a village. My village is crazy amazing. I am grateful. I am blessed. I need a box of Kleenex.

About Elaine Tan Comeau

Photo: Ron Comeau

Elaine Tan Comeau is an enterprising mom of three, wife to the smartest and kindest man she knows, a life-long learner, woman of faith, traveler, foodie, keynote speaker, #1 Best Selling Author, Multi-Award-Winning Entrepreneur and Educator, CEO and Founder of one of *Dragons' Den* favorite pitches, Easy Daysies®!

Easy Daysies Ltd. incited a bidding war among all five investors, which also became one of the show's Top Five Most Heart Warming Pitches, and was also chosen by Ford Company as one the 2014 *Dragons' Den* Driven For Success Companies that exemplified Ford's Four Pillars of Success. Elaine has been featured in *Forbes*, *Financial Post*, *Maclean's*, *Canadian Business*, *Huffington Post*, Global News, CBC, CTV, ABC, FOX32 News, to name a few.

She is a sought-after speaker and writer, sharing her expertise with entrepreneurs, educators, and parents on radio, television, and for text books like *Educational Psychology*. She is passionate about coming alongside women entrepreneurs and cheering them on to take action to achieve success! Hear her strategies on her podcast called *Elaine's Kitchen Table... The Business of Real Life* (www.ElainesKitchenTable.com). Elaine is raved about in many entrepreneurial books, including Kevin O'Leary's and Jim Treliving's latest books. She is proud to be an Ambassador for Mompreneurs® Canada, recipient of the Chamber of Commerce Award for Excellence in Business, the 2014 Canadian Mompreneur of the Year, and be named one of the 2018 Top Ten Most Innovative Companies by Small Business British Columbia.

Book Elaine to Speak

Book Elaine Tan Comeau as your Keynote Speaker and you are guaranteed to make your event inspirational, motivational and highly entertaining, as Elaine will challenge your audience to take action in a talk that will induce laughter, and possibly tears!

Photo: Anthony Goto

For over a decade, Elaine Tan Comeau has been invited to speak to female entrepreneurs, educators, parents, and kid entrepreneurs too!

For more info and to book Elaine for your next event, visit www.ElainesKitchenTable.com, or e-mail elaine@elaineskitchentable.com.

Made in the USA
San Bernardino, CA
17 March 2019